50

SHADES

OF

GRACE

50 SHADES OF GRACE

An intriguing examination of self and purpose through this heartwarming tale of a single lady ▪ chance encounters ▪ supernatural love▪ and the favor of grace

•

T. T. CAROLE

ABFL Books (a division of Weekend Wonders)
SAINT LOUIS, MISSOURI
Est. 2018

© 2018 T. T. Carole

All rights reserved. No part of this publication may be reproduced, stored in a retrieval system, or transmitted in any form or by any means—electronic, mechanical, photocopy, recording, scanning or any other—except for concise quotations in critical reviews or articles, without prior written permission of the publisher.

Published in St. Louis, Missouri by ABFL Books. ABFL Books is a division of Weekend Wonders, a sole proprietorship.

Website: www.abeautyfilledlife.com

Publisher's Note: This is a work of fiction. Names, characters, places, and incidents are a product of the author's imagination. Locales and public names are sometimes used for atmospheric purposes. Any resemblance to actual people, living or dead, or to businesses, companies, events, institutions, or locales is completely coincidental.

Unless otherwise indicated, Scripture references and / or quotations are taken from the "Holy Bible, New International Version", ©1973, 1978, 1984, by International Bible Society. Used by permission of 'Zondervan. All rights reserved.

Book Layout © 2017 BookDesignTemplates.com

ISBN 978-1-7322927-3-1

Library of Congress Cataloging-in-Publication Data
T. T. Carole, 1962
50 shades of grace / T. T. Carole
Summary: "Helpful coaching for single ladies and women in need of encouragement." – Provided by publisher.

1. Self Help—Adult Fiction; 2. Christian Life—Adult Fiction; 3. Romance—Adult Fiction; 4. Singles--Adult Fiction; 5. Single Women—Adult Fiction; 6. Inspirational—Adult Fiction; 7. Study Guide—Adult Fiction

To the loving memory of my parents (Henry, 1980 & Viana 2005) who gifted me with a good name and solid foundation from which to launch at my appointed time.

I Thank God for allowing me a very special and intimate relationship and fellowship with Him.

Also, a special "Thank You" to my family and close circle of friends (you know who you are) who are always so supportive of my many projects and whims.

I can truly say from the depths of my heart that you all are simply the best!

"We delight in the beauty of the butterfly, but rarely admit the changes it has gone through to achieve that beauty."

MAYA ANGELOU

Contents

Preface i

Chapter 1 1

The Sophisticated Lady 1

   An Ornament of Grace 3

Chapter 2 7

The Ratcheted Encounter 7

Chapter 3 13

Let the Games Begin 13

Chapter 4 21

He Had Her at Hello 21

   One for the Road 23

Chapter 5 27

Ready for Action 27

   Everything Going as Planned 28

Chapter 6 35

The Screeching Halt! 35

Chapter 7 43

Grace - The Total Package 43

Girl's Imagination Gone Wild..44

Fifty 46

Expressions of Beauty 48

Pardon the Interruption... 50

The Craving 51

The Obsession 52

Redeeming Grace..56

The Gift of Grace 59

APPENDIX - A Guide for Personal Application 63

   Discussion Questions for Chapter 1 64

   Discussion Questions for Chapter 2............................65

   Discussion Questions for Chapter 3............................66

   Discussion Questions for Chapter 4............................67

   Discussion Questions for Chapter 5........................... 68

   Discussion Questions for Chapter 6............................69

   Discussion Questions for Chapter 7........................... 70

About The Author..73

Also From T. T. CAROLE...75

Contact Information 77

Preface

On any given day, a lovely lady of any age, status, or persuasion might start her day in a benignly routine manner. She awakes either instinctively according to her internal clock, or to the sound of an alarm of one sort or another. She gets out of bed—or off the sofa (fully dressed in the previous day's attire, if it were one of those devil-may-care evenings)—either with a joyful bolt, or grudgingly—one body part at a time. Either way, she went to sleep knowing what it is that she either wants to do, or must do in the coming day, and whenever she wakes, she prepares herself accordingly. There are days, however, when no amount of preparation can ready her for the manner of storm that is heading her way.

Saved, single, or satisfied, she sat alone at a table in the banquet hall—or so she thought—while waiting for the start of a wedding ceremony, set to take place later that Saturday afternoon. Distracted by her own thoughts, she did not see him sitting there, nor did she notice or give thought to the fact that she was the object of another's affection.

Eventually, the fella who—in her mind—she nicknamed Mr. Wonderful, managed to get her attention in the most unconventional way. He was a looker; however, his first words to her left her not knowing whether to laugh or cry.

As the conversation between them ensued during the afternoon, there was an undeniable connection between the two of them; yet, there was the presence of another in the room whose desire for her was even more pure and yet unassuming.

As the afternoon progressed, one thing led to another, and she soon became like putty in his hands—or was she? She sensed that he was up to something; but, at the same time, she could not get enough of him. She did whatever she thought it would take to entice him into staying close or coming back for more.

His last visit, though, proved to be too much. Something was off; he began asking prying questions that ripped into her well-manicured psyche and started to make her feel very uncomfortable. She was not prepared for him to slay her, merely, with his words. But it happened, and he ran away and left her in a puddle.

Then, just as she was about to become totally unraveled, that mysterious one in the room (who kept watch over her during the entire encounter) approached; swooping in to offer words of wisdom and comfort that would save her from her negative self.

Like the many characters in her head, the mysterious visitor—who was an indescribable beauty—engulfs the lovely lady with her love, which leaves her feeling restored and reassured.

Before letting her go, the lovely lady asks, "Who are you? What shall I call you?" Then, never breaking eye contact and before sauntering away, she turned and said, "My name is Grace."

Chapter 1

The Sophisticated Lady

It all started on an enchanting, very warm (but not too hot), late summer afternoon. She had arrived several hours early to the rented banquet hall, not only to attend, but to also serve as coordinator-in-chief (if needed) for her niece's wedding. There were others tarrying in the room, but she sat at a table comfortably and alone (so she thought) and was in part dabbling in social media on her phone, and in part watching the decorator who was working feverishly to add finishing touches to the room. Darting back and forth in her mind—she watched some; complimented some; analyzed some; and imagined alternative settings some. All this while, deep in her heart, hoping for the best.

So, there she sat at that moment in time. She is a strong, determined, educated, professional woman. She is also a woman of faith who is careful to in no ways conflate what she is with who she is. Her attire is very fashionable, and by some standards, she is a better than average-looking woman of a certain age.

T. T. Carole

Though on the lower end of the spectrum she was still a baby boomer, and everybody knows that boomers are notoriously guilty of ignoring or trying to evade middle age. Nevertheless, at that moment she was the epitome of that 'sophisticated lady' that famous composers or performers write songs or sing about.

As such; to some, the 'sophisticated lady' is a fierce, independent-thinking, smart and classy lady who—despite her secret fears and insecurities—appears to have it all together in every facet of life, thus making other ladies aspire to be her. And then to some she is a sharp-tongued, good-looking, feisty chick who is not afraid to go for what she wants but nevertheless ends up as nothing more than a fantasy, or the object of someone's desire. And yet; to some, the 'sophisticated lady' is one who, once scorned by love, tries to get even for her hurts by chasing fancies and causing others pain; all while—deep inside—still saddened by her losses and sinking further into despair.

Therefore, any lady bearing the 'sophisticated lady' label could be a very complex individual who is like a modern-day Cinderella.

In the beloved Cinderella fairytale, Cinderella sings a song about sitting in her own little chair in her own little corner of the world. There, she sings, she can be whatever it is that she can imagine. She could imagine herself more beautiful and instantly become the most beautiful girl in the world. She could imagine herself more adventurous and find herself in places—exciting and unknown. She could imagine herself more fearless and standing face-to-face with danger; or more carefree—doing things she would not otherwise do and making brave decisions that she would not otherwise make.

Cinderella lived boldly and fearlessly in her imaginations because she knew that so long as she was only imagining those things—if something really spooked her—she could cease the imaginings and return to her real-life, little chair--nicely tucked away in an obscure corner of a room in a secure home.

Therefore, taking the imaginary approach to life not only yielded for her opportunities to live out her dreams, but it also kept her safe from both inside and outside forces. Her imagining, for her, was a type of coping mechanism.

As for the modern-day Cinderella—whether she is waiting for her prince to come; or realizing that her king has been with her all along—a lady bearing the 'sophisticated lady' label might be one who has decided that her best coping mechanism is to construct her own facade, act out her own realities, and making sure that she has a safe place to run to when things start to get too scary.

As for the type of person who might bear the 'sophisticated lady' label; she is not one, she is many, and her main goal is to do whatever it takes to make it through the day.

An Ornament of Grace

A snapshot of that moment in time on that warm afternoon would reveal this lovely lady as a woman at the precipice of womanhood. She did not arrive there by surprise; the journey over the years to that destination needed a lot of considerations. In fact, along the way, she was always unconsciously conscious of her independence; even in her 20s.

By the time she entered her 30s (even while the deafening and unnerving sound of the imaginary, yet infamous biological clock was ticking like the sound of a jack hammer chipping away at a pillar of stone) she had even trained her mother to stop asking her about marrying and having children. She did this simply by not marrying or having kids.

Just to be clear, the lovely lady had neither an aversion to marriage nor (in all its glory) to bearing children; she just never made doing these a priority in her life.

As such, time moved on and before she knew it, she had graciously accepted and settled into life as she knows it now. She was comfortable with living her life to the fullest and she entertained only fleeting thoughts of the 'what could have been(s)'.

So, by all indications, the lovely lady had it all together. She lived comfortably. She knew how to take care of business, how to bat down incoming storms to hold things together—no matter what—and most of all, how to take care of herself. That, of course, was until she met the fresh young man whose invasion into her life not only rivaled, but even surpassed the kind and well-intended, but arduous, sentiments of her mother's.

Yet; at that moment in time, there she sat, cloaked in her own illustrious world, not knowing that a storm that packed gale-force winds that could (if possible) blow her tightly-held, well-coifed facade right away, was brewing on the horizon.

However; for a split second, when she took a blink break from her busyness, the lovely lady caught a glimpse of another, who tarried about, but in a more unique way than the others.

The aura caused her to pause for just a second, until an alert from one of the apps on her android once again wrestled her attention away.

Yet, even though she looked away, she could not fully shake the thought of the other.

Chapter 2

The Ratcheted Encounter

More members of the wedding party and a few guests are still slowly trickling into the banquet hall. Someone from across the room calls out her name while rushing away. The lovely lady looks over and sees the bride's mother moving hastily toward the back room with a garment bag strewn across her shoulder and a rolling piece of luggage in tow.

"Hello-o-o-o, latey bird," she responded teasingly. Realizing that she, too, would soon have to go to the back to see if she could be of assistance, she looked back down to continue to get a rundown and read reviews of movies that were coming and going for the upcoming month on her streaming channels.

As she began swiping more hurriedly to the left, right, up, and down, she stumbled across a preview of a movie that she was interested in watching.

She watched the trailer and then began reading the mixed reviews—some great; some not so great. When she began analyzing one particularly detailed review that was deftly pointing out what the movie got right and what it got wrong, someone stirred.

He must have been sitting there the whole time; but distracted by her own thoughts, she obviously paid him no mind. However, whenever he spoke, and the lovely lady looked over to see his face, then all bets were off.

First there was a couple of quick glances. Then the glances led to a longer gaze.

In her quick assessment she noticed that he was short in stature but mostly average in size.

She blushed a little as she got a glimpse of his rich, smooth, bronze complexion; his beautiful hazel-brown eyes; and his deeply dimpled cheeks—assets that almost any woman would find irresistible.

She also noticed that he had a serious demeanor. And, it did not take much studying him before she detected that his conversation was stern and about as straight-forward and honest as anyone would ever hope.

In fact, his first words to her were: "I gotta pee!"

> HER: You have to what? (While thinking to herself, 'this guy does not have a filter').
> HIM: I gotta pee.
> HER: Then go pee. Do you know where the restroom is?
> HIM: Yes, it's over there.
> HER: Okay, so what? Do you need somebody to go in there with you?
> HIM: Yeah, I do.

HER:	*Then go find somebody and ask them to go with you!*
HIM:	*Okay.*

Then the guy to whom she sarcastically affixed the often-overused and sometimes overstated moniker, 'Mr. Wonderful', loped off into the proverbial sunset, running off to handle his business.

In the meantime, while sitting there and unintentionally regurgitating the earlier conversation, the lovely lady sat bemused; not knowing whether to laugh or cry.

In her heart, she is impressed by his innocence and openness and, at the same time, shocked to life by his bluntness and unsolicited willingness to share.

She looked down to continue reading the critique about the movie, which happened to be the adaptation of the book of Ruth: "... and as is almost always is the case, the writers took too much creative license and—though engaging—muddied the storyline and veered away from the original intent of the tale", the reviewer opined.

Without seeing the movie, the lovely lady took the reviewer's opinion into consideration, and being the creative type that she is, reflectively, began fantasizing about how she would guide the actors to depict the main characters and their storylines—if she were directing.

For the matriarch, Naomi—the lovely lady mused—she would choose for the part, an actor who is not only a ripened beauty, but one who can bring great depth to her scenes.

She would encourage the actor in her portrayal of this woman of strength and dignity to allow herself to sway with merriment while at home enjoying her family even while tucked away in a foreign land. And, she would urge her to allow herself to cry ugly and bellow with as much pain, brokenness as one can humanly feel, in the scenes where Naomi is devastated by and dealing with the grief of losing her husband, both sons, and her home. Further, she would push the actor to tenderly expose the assurance of Naomi's faith, courage, and wisdom as she is rising from the sands and finding healing in her brokenness. Finally, she would energize her to shout on the inside with boldness and confidence while making decisions about her life and the lives of the ones she loves and bracing for what the future might bring.

"Hey auntie," a voice interrupted. It was her nephew hauling in a box of chafing dishes filled with prepared food. "Where do you want this?"

"Set them on the round table in the corner for now; the servers have not yet dressed the food tables", she replied.

Interrupted from her directing job, she once again turned her attention to darting back and forth between the decorator who was (at the time) twirling what seemed like tons of tulle while trying to perfect the backdrop for the alter; and her eyes looking down at her phone (scrolling through more of the review). Then suddenly, she catches a glimpse of Mr. Wonderful walking briskly across the room and making his way back to the table.

As he approached, she noticed he seemed more joyful and confident than when he left. He must have had time for reflection during the time he was away.

Her guess was that to him, if she could understand his most base need, then she most definitely was someone with whom he wanted a deeper conversation—or something.

And, as the seconds ticked away, it was obvious that she had become for him, a person of interest. In fact, it was not long after Mr. Wonderful landed back in the seat he had previously left, that he leaned in to start a conversation.

It was not long after that, that in a serendipitous moment that seemed created by a fairytale-like twinkling of the eye, the lovely lady and Mr. Wonderful sat face-to-face at the table, communicating with each other in an unforced manner. This, at least for her, is turning out to be a very intriguing time.

As Mr. Wonderful engaged the lovely lady in a more remarkable conversation that lasted longer than his prior brash, unfiltered proclamation, she could not help but notice that his voice was neither too high nor too low; but kind of firm, soft, and sweet.

However, even as she detected that his grammar was a little questionable at times, she appreciated his modulation and almost-perfect pitch.

Yet, as intrigued as she had become, she cautiously sensed that there was something more to his conversation, so she wisely decided that she must watch him very carefully, but not too provocatively.

Strangely though, while engaged in the conversation, the lovely lady, yet again, could sense that someone was watching over her.

T. T. Carole

The eyes felt familiar as they seemed to envelope her whole being. She quickly scanned the room but could not make a connection. Then quickly, her mind's eye caught a glimpse of one who had previously given a wink and a nod.

Chapter 3

Let the Games Begin

As she and Mr. Wonderful continued to dally in their dazzling conversation, the lovely lady continued to delicately conceal her uneasiness about all that she was sensing. She managed to disguise her conflicting feelings about their rapport, and the story she was weaving together in her head about him, by steeling her mind to remain confident of her grasp and her understanding of the situation. She willed herself to take hold of the fact that no matter how slick he thought he was, Mr. Wonderful was not the only person in the room with insight about the game that he might have been trying to play.

Over the span of her adult life, the lovely lady often fell before as prey to many of his type. And, though most of the outcomes of those encounters were enlightening, some did not fare so well.

Therefore, since experience has proved a great teacher, she relied on memories (the good, bad, and ugly) to inform her about what to look for to weed out the less desirables.

Yet even so, the lovely lady was not immune to being swept away by good looks and enjoyable conversation.

Quick! She needed to regain her composure. To make a graceful exit, the lovely lady excused herself from the table to go to the powder room. However, she could only linger there for so long, she thought, before her absence appeared an obvious attempt to escape.

Yet after finishing her business and fixing her makeup; while giving her hands a final wash, she looked up into the mirror, and there was either something about the soft soothing feel of the soap or the temperature of the water on her hands that caused her to linger there.

Then, she once again, started imagining how she would direct the movie she had started a short while ago. Her focus, this time, was drawn to Orpah: "... the other daughter-in-law, could easily have been just a piece of furniture. They did not give her much of a role...," she remembered reading in the review.

"So, who was Orpah and what did Orpah want?" the lovely lady pondered. As she gleaned from what she knew about the Biblical version of the story in her head, she began putting together a profile of Orpah's appearance and attributes.

She remembered that Orpah was young and though not yet a mother, was of childbearing age. She imagined her as an innocent young lady; joyful, newly married, and excited about the prospect of starting a family.

Therefore, she imagined Orpah to be, as beautiful as Naomi, but much younger.

She imagined her petite in size and with eyes that seem to sparkle.

Then, she recalled how after the loss of her husband, Orpah clung to her mother-in-law, and both experienced much pain.

She recalled reading the conversation that Orpah had with the very broken Naomi whenever Naomi desperately decided to move back to her homeland.

She also remembered reading that even though Orpah was loyal to Naomi and had at first expressed a desire to leave with her, that at Naomi's urging, Orpah chose between the family she lost and the one that might exist for her in the future. Orpah chose to stay and fight for her heart's desire.

The lovely lady then decided that Orpah's character should depict an unshakeable determination and a quiet resolve.

Her thoughts—now—interrupted again as the creaking door began opening wider as someone was entering.

The lovely lady felt pleased, however, about how the movie was going in her head; she was excited for—and empowered by—the idea of highlighting the characters' strengths and weaknesses. But she realized that she had to go back to the table and face her own reality that was in the making.

"Where have you been?" he demanded gently as she made it back to her seat.

"I told you I had to go to the restroom. I am a girl. It takes us longer to do stuff in there," she teased.

They picked up the conversation near where they had left off with relative ease, and she remained mesmerized by the encounter; however, at the same time, she was actively sizing him up and her instincts eventually paid off.

Though time was passing, she was enjoying herself so much, it seemed suspended.

But after slowly hearing, then yielding to her inside voice that was telling her that she had run into his type many times before, she knew to watch his eyes to figure out when he was ready to make his move.

She studied him closely and before she could finish the thought, her fears about him materialized. She managed to notice the exact moment that he set his hazel-brown eyes on her precious possessions. Then, his next move confirmed her instincts! He was the type to go straight for the goods.

"What's that?" He asked bluntly. "What's what?" she demurred. "That," he said as he pointed questionably. "You mean my purse? It's a purse," she said while thinking 'he had better take a better approach than that.'

She thought that at this point he had realized the silliness of his question... or maybe not. Or, he was just trying to throw her of off her game just a little bit more.

But as some who are aficionadas of a familiar idiomatic expression would say: game recognizes game.

"Let the games begin,' she laughed in her mind.

Her shock at his line of questioning was of no effect on him, and he persisted. "What's in there?"

At this point the lovely lady is thinking, "Oh, we are going to continue down this path, huh? Okay, I will play."

Then she answered him very sweetly, saying, "You know, just girl stuff."

That moment seemed to have added fuel to the fire, and the conversation continued to turn for the worse:

> HIM: Girl stuff! What kind of girl stuff?
> HER: You know, like makeup, lotion, tissue. Stuff like that.
> HIM: Makeup? What's makeup?
> HER: Well ...lipstick, powder, lip gloss. Stuff like that.
> HIM: What else do you got in there?
> HER: Well, my driver's license and my wallet are in there too.

He was obviously on an expedition, fishing for something else, and she guessed that he sensed that she was holding back. But since game recognizes game, they both continued playing. All the while, she is growing more amused and he is becoming slightly more frustrated. He then paused for a about half a minute and then asked simply and very politely, "Can I look in your purse?"

Regrettably, either his frustration riled him, or he thought he had found an opening.

He then went in for the kill.

> HER: And why do you want to look in my purse?
> HIM: To see what you are holding.

"What respectable lady would let a stranger go through her purse? No, buster; that is a road too far!" she thought.

She was not having it—not if he were the Prince of Wales, and not even if she were desperately trying to spare his feelings, and at the same time, salvage what she thought was the beginning of a budding relationship.

Therefore, to balance going off on an indignant rant and keeping her composure so as not to run him away, she quickly came up with a more gracious move. She promptly grabbed her purse from the table and fished around on the inside to see if she could find for him the delectable pleasure that he wanted.

Before too long the smitten, but slightly panicked, lovely lady teasingly, unveiled to Mr. Wonderful the fruits of her fetch.

HER: Is this what you want?
HIM: Yes. Yes, can I have it?
HER: Which one do you want?
HIM: All of it!

All of it?

Once again, Mr. Wonderful did not hold back. With those three little words, he let the lovely lady know that he played the game to win, and at that moment, he must have felt that he had done just that.

Surprisingly though, the lovely lady was not the least bit incensed by his honesty; in fact, she was quite amused.

But even in her amusement, she realized that he was not going to stop there; there was sure to be more to come. That thought led her to wonder in silence what she should do to prepare herself; however, before she tried to answer her own question, she felt something like a tap on her shoulder or a whisper in her ear.

She sensed that someone passing by was aiming to distract her.

Chapter 4

He Had Her at Hello

Time passed. It seemed like forever, but it really was not that long. People were still trickling in. The beautiful bride peeked in to say hello. The caterer and servers were setting up the food. And, the lovely lady and Mr. Wonderful were talking about everything. She learned of the names of his siblings and other family members, the foods he loves and the ones he hates, his go-to toys, and more importantly the kinds of goodies that he wished she would buy for him. 'Wait! How did we get here?' she thought. 'Things are moving way too fast!'

As they continued their exchange, a young lady came from the back to deliver a message to him causing an abrupt interruption.

The lovely lady did not want to hear anything not intended for her ears, so she politely got up from her seat and went up to the make-shift alter to speak with the decorator.

This was a perfect opportunity to express her satisfaction with how beautifully things were shaping up, and (since she was working alone) to offer to help.

They chatted for a few minutes and the decorator, who introduced herself as Katie, accepted the compliment but graciously declined the help. The lovely lady, looking back at the table (she had left her purse there) noticed Mr. Wonderful was nowhere in sight.

She ended the courteous chitchat with Katie and nervously headed back to her seat. Upon her return, she found that things were just as she had left them, but he was not there.

"Where is he and why do I care?" she wondered. She also wondered how it is possible for her to not even notice him before their first exchange, and now she cannot seem to shake him. That brought to her mind a line from the Jerry McGuire movie and she agreed: he had her at hello—or the other thing he said.

Sitting alone once again, she realized it is still early, and it looked like everything was running smoothly thus far.

She previously offered to help the decorator but there was no need; and she had not received any calls for help from the back room, so she assumed there was no need there either.

Then, she remembered that she forgot to pick up a card for the wedding couple and thought that now would be a good time to run out to the nearest drug store to pick one up.

Settled in her mind that this was a great idea, she grabbed her purse and headed out the door.

One for the Road

It was a little warmer outside now than it was when she first arrived. So, not wanting to spend too much time soaking up the sun, she walked briskly across the lot to her car.

Sitting comfortably in the car—air blasting—she was on her way to find the perfect card for the happy couple. Ironically, when she tuned the radio to her favorite, oldies station, the song that happened to be playing was the O'Jays version of "Now That We Found Love".

Rocking in her seat (hands firmly on the steering wheel), she sang along as the chorus to the song asked, "Now that we found love what are we gonna do with it?"

The lovely lady beamed, not for herself, but for the wedding that was about to take place. She knew that her niece had made it one of her most important goals in life to not only get married, but to marry a man she loved. Today was the day. Today Ashley was marrying her friend and her love. Though, after the song ended, her sentimental feelings caused her mind to wander.

'I wonder what that is like,' she wondered. She did not want to become muddled in those thoughts, so she directed her attention back to the scenes that she had yet to finish in the movie that she was directing in her mind. She was pleased with her treatment of Naomi's and Orpah' characters, thus far, so she turned her thoughts to the book's namesake—Ruth.

She could not pull up the movie reviewer's notes on her phone because she was driving at the time; however, she did recall that she thought the comment about Ruth's portrayal (if written and acted in such a way) was harsh but well deserved.

The critic based their opinion on scenes where Ruth's character was less than gracious toward the Boaz character. If that were the case, then the lovely lady could not help agreeing with the critic. Then she began creating the character.

She imagined Ruth to be like a beautiful, blooming flower, and who, unbeknownst to her, would soon be nurtured and then harvested according to her higher purpose. And, like Orpha, Ruth was a raven-haired beauty—young, energetic, and primed to start a family of her own—but who also witnessed fate dash her hopes and dreams when her husband, too, died too soon.

She recalled that the critic (who wrote the review) suggested that in the movie, Ruth's character portrayal presented a woman who was sassy or quick-witted in her dealings with others.

The lovely lady agreed with the critic that the portrayal was not in line with the original story. In fact, her recollection of Ruth led her to believe that if Ruth did in fact have a gritty streak at all, she only put it on display in terms of her loyalty, resilience, and pure determination to carry on.

"That is what Ruth's character should exude," she thought. She was careful, though, not to require that Ruth—in following her mother-in-law to her home land (one that was foreign to her in their beliefs and customs)—was more loyal than Orpah—who chose to stay home.

Instead, she wanted to magnify the ideal that Ruth's decision was based on something that stirred deep inside of her—something that she was not readily aware.

She wanted to show that Ruth's surrender—not only unto her own current, devastating set of circumstances but also to Naomi's faith—sealed her destiny, and it was at that point, that fate came rushing in on her like a raging storm. She thought it was important to emphasize that at that point, Ruth had no other choice.

'Wow!' she thought as she turned onto the lot. 'The lot is nearly empty. Where are people hanging out on this (albeit) early, but warm, sunny afternoon?"

The lovely lady exited her car and went into the store to search for that perfect card. It was not long after she went to the card aisle that she found it; a ready-made card that was somehow customized to express her exact sentiments.

While heading to the check-out, she realized that she was walking past an aisle where she could find a special gift for that new man in her life (even if only for a moment). She stopped so fast that she might have created skid marks on the floor.

She went down the aisle and before she knew it, she had spent more than fifteen minutes in that aisle, while trying to find for him the perfect gift.

Pacing back and forth, she finally narrowed it down to two choices; then thoughtfully picked one of the two.

Satisfied with her purchases, she got back into the car and headed back to the banquet hall. She did not know if it was due to her excitement about her purchase, or her anticipation of how he might react when he sees it, but the ride back to the hall seemed much shorter than the ride to the store.

Chapter 5

Ready for Action

The atmosphere in the banquet hall seems different from when she had left it; more people had trickled in and it was busier, but the table where the magic was beginning to happen remained empty and undisturbed. Then, by the time she was about to take her seat, she looked up to see Mr. Wonderful almost skipping across the room to greet her. "I was looking for you," he said nervously. Without telling him where she had been, she said, "Well, I am back now. What's on your mind?" They both smiled, she thought, at his inquisitiveness and her sassiness. And, before she knew it, they had both taken their seats and started a new conversation. All the while, knowing the surprise that she was planning to spring on him, nothing—not the decorator, apps, or activities on her phone, nor any daydreams—could distract her from the delightful tête-à-tête. However, she had no way of knowing that this was a precursor to either an innocent, spontaneous moment of chaos, or a well-planned setup.

The new conversation was not that new at all because; though said slightly differently, there were a considerable number of reiterations of the same topics discussed during their earlier exchanges.

Nevertheless, they managed to keep the banter lively and interesting. Then, as her excitement about the find that she picked up for him started to bubble within her, the lovely lady interrupted her dubiously named Mr. Wonderful in mid-thought and while smiling broadly said, "I have something for you."

She watched as his beautiful, hazel-brown eyes opened to what seemed as wide as saucers, and if possible would have bathed the whole room with a warm amber light.

She heard the glee in his voice as he asked excitedly, "What is it?"

In her mind, even that sight dulled in comparison to how he would react whenever she would present him with a gift that she had no doubt would make him (as some would say) 'as pleased as punch.

So, without her usual teasing and hesitation, she reached into her purse and then made the presentation.

It was just as she had expected. His reaction was priceless. Yet, she kept her wits about her as she decided to not give it all to him at one time because she wanted to make sure that no matter whatever was happening or wherever he went in the room, he would always have to come back to her for more.

Everything Going as Planned

Mr. Wonderful was certainly pleased with his gift. Moreover, the lovely lady was pleased that her calculation to string him along by controlling when and how of much it she would let him have at one time, was brilliant.

This, she thought, would keep him beholden to her for as long as she wanted his attention.

But, something in her plan broke.

Her Mr. Wonderful kept the lovely lady in his sights for much of the afternoon—even after breaking away for a short while to speak with different acquaintances.

He then returned to the table, but this time not asking for more, but venturing to start a whole new conversation; one that was sure to put the lovely lady on edge.

In making his move, he curiously reared back in his chair; licked his fingers; smiled broadly, and looked deep into the lovely lady's eyes and asked operatically: "How old are you?"

> HER: I am not going to tell you that.
> HIM: Why not?
> HER: Because you do not need to know.
> HIM: Yes, I do. How old is you?
> HER: How old are you?
> HIM: I'm 5.
> HER: You are 5? How old do you think I am?
> HIM: I don't know...21?
> HER: You think I am 21? That is so sweet; now let us leave it at that.
> HIM: But how old is you for real?
> HER: If I tell you, you are going to think I am really old.
> HIM: No, I won't. How old is you?
> HER: You mean 'how old are you?'
> HIM: Yes, how old are you?

Feeling uneasy about his insistence, but comfortable enough in the relationship they had formed to share more about herself, she told him the unfiltered truth.

In her heart she knew he would respond in some kind of way, but at the same time, she was unprepared for how he would deliver his response.

To her amazement, little Mr. Wonderful, looked down and away, then back up and over at her (with the most sheepish grin he could muster) and said, "Yeah, you are pretty old". "Just think," she thought; "not only did I give you gummy worms, but I gave you extra sour gummy worms!"

Nevertheless, they continued their conversation. Why end it now? She found him very entertaining and he knew that she had a bag full of his favorite candy. And, though (as more people started filing into the hall) he would spot a familiar face and run off from time-to-time; he always returned. However, each of his times away lasted a little longer than the last.

During what she thought would be his last run (because it was getting close to the time that he would have to be dressed for his role in the wedding), the lovely lady had time to continue her musing about her version of the award-winning 'Story of Ruth' movie that she was rewriting in her head. So, while sitting there and feeling grateful for being in such an energizing environment at a wonderful time as this, she turned her attention to the one in the story who symbolizes hope, restoration, and fulfillment: she directed her attention to Boaz.

It was Boaz who came to the aid of Naomi and Ruth in their most desperate times. Though he did not run to their aid whenever he learned that Naomi and her daughter-in-law had returned, destitute, to Naomi's homeland; however, with a watchful eye, he perceived the problems that had beset them. He also noticed the way that they cared for each other and how they conducted themselves around the other women (and men) in the land, and he was pleased. Therefore, whenever Naomi and Ruth forged their plan to seek his help, Boaz was more than accommodating.

Boaz's generosities restored them. His loving kindnesses gave them a new hope for the future. His name reinstated for them the honor they had lost. Moreover, his guidance set them on course with their destiny.

In considering all of that, the lovely lady thought about what Boaz's physical attributes would be. Is he to be so handsome—sporting dark, thick, curly hair; strong, chiseled features; and a long, lean, well-sculptured body—that all the maidens would desire him? "No," she thought; she did not want that to be his story.

Then, is he to be a virile, young buck who is inexperienced like Orpah and Ruth, or an older man who is full of wisdom like Naomi? "Hum--either is possible but only one is probable," she thought.

Then after a little more, careful consideration, she decided that looks-wise, her Boaz character should be so uniquely nondescript that he could be whatever someone needed in their heart for him to be.

"Hey, lil' sis", her brother bellowed from across the room, causing a break in her moment of intense concentration. She looked over and waved as he (walking with a sense of nervous pride) made his way to the back. No time for chit-chat; it was his baby girl's big day and he knew it.

Somehow with that exchange, she dropped her guard, and the lovely lady began experiencing a moment of sadness. "What's happening?" she wondered. Then, as if to answer her own question, she realized that the 'what ifs' were creeping in and starting to invade her psyche. However, before she could let that drag her deeper into her emotions, she noticed movement from the mysterious lady in the room; it was an odd sway as from this way to that.

Consequently, trying to come to grips with the thoughts that were invading her mind and, at the same time, processing the peculiar movements of the mysterious lady across the room, proved to be enough to distract her from both.

She shook them both off, and while still sitting alone at the table, she went back to the story she was drafting in her head.

Coming back to herself, the lovely lady circled back to the critic's review of the movie, and she read his or her opinion that the ending of the movie was—in a way—anti-climactic.

"How can that be?" she asked herself while feeling overwhelmed by the suggestion. "How can the ending of this story be anti-climactic? Who does that?" she thought. She then re-imagined her version of the ending of the story, and in doing so, she imagined how she would present each character in the end.

She imagined that Naomi—who was so devastated by the situation that was thrust upon her life that she changed her name to one that means 'a bitter woman'—can now (through her relations with Boaz and her daughter-in-law) become a grandma and bounce a baby on her knee. She was no longer bitter, but now restored and fulfilled.

And, she imagined that though Orpah was scantly mentioned again, she is now living in her homeland, happily married, and expecting a family of her own.

Then, she imagined life pampering Ruth as she is recovering from the emotional scars of the tragedies she faced earlier in life, and the physical scars she suffered during the back-breaking times she spent sowing and reaping in the fields as she was trying to support her broken mother-in-law. And, she further imagined for Ruth that because a circle of sisters and others prayed for as much, she would live victoriously and as one who would help to build nations.

Finally, she imagined that Boaz—though he already had a good reputation and had amassed riches and land—celebrated added acclaim rewarded to him for his unselfish and purposeful acts of coming to the aid of two devastated ladies (at the appointed time) and thus, being instrumental in setting everything on a more promising path. He, along with Ruth, were on course for building great nations.

The lovely lady's mind briefly drifted away from the story as she applauded how (though sometimes painful) life seemed to have unfolded for Naomi, Ruth, Boaz, and Orpah according to a well-orchestrated plan.

"That was then, but what about now?" she wondered. "Is it possible that what we perceive to be our tragedies are really episodes of veiled joy? Are our uncertainties really opportunities for more faith? Does our surrender to a situation result in a dance with destiny? If those are truths, then how do we better equip ourselves to handle those truths?" she wondered.

"Girl, you are going way too deep," she teased, before she turned her attention back to her story. "I need to do the ending."

For an epic ending that would hush the critics, the lovely lady imagined the movie would end with the sounds of Ruth in labor, giving birth to hers and Boaz's son. After the baby cries, the camera shows a glimpse of the faces of Naomi and then Ruth as they cry tears of joy, and then Boaz as he beams with pride. The baby, wrapped in cloth, is kicking, and screaming in wonderment—he is now a stranger in this whole new world. The scene darkens, then with a magnificent flash, Boaz, Ruth, and Naomi are standing—victoriously—far away, on a hill. They are—as spectators—watching a story unfold. They are looking down and witnessing the birth of new generations and the building of great, new nations.

The credits roll; trumpets are blowing triumphantly; the wind catches a tear from the eyes of Boaz and whips it around and turns it into a storm, symbolizing the many trials that are yet to come before all things are set to right...

"A little over the top?" she thought. "Maybe so, but at least it is not anti-climactic."

Chapter 6

The Screeching Halt!

A little more than an hour and a half had passed since she first entered the banquet hall. Yet, without giving thought to the moments when it seemed she were suspended in time while conversing with Mr. Wonderful; her producing the 'Story of Ruth' movie in her mind; or her scampering to and from the drug store for a card, the lovely lady happened to notice the clock on the wall and wondered, 'Wow! Where does time go?' Even so, with more adults either working in various roles in the room and more children huddling and running around in the back, the room seemed busier than ever. She looked back to see if she could spot little Mr. Wonderful, and then in an instant, he must have caught her stare and he came swooning back in for more conversation and candy, of course.

There was something a little different about him this time. Either he was suffering from an incredible sugar high or his cavorting with his contemporaries in the back of the room supercharged him in an unexpected way. He questioned her in a more pointed way this time. And, to her living horror, the lovely lady realized that everything preceding the next few upcoming moments was a calm before the storm. Gently catching his breath and clutching a few sour worms in his hand, he started a conversation anew.

HIM: You have any kids?
HER: No.
HIM: Why not?
HER: Because I do not, that is all.
HIM: But why not? You need some kids.
HER: Well, not everybody will have kids.
HIM: Yes, some do!
HER: Well, some do not.
HIM: Yes, some do!
HER: I know some do, but some do not, and that is okay (thinking, "oh mercy").
HIM: Yes, some do!
HER: I know, but for various reasons, not everybody will have kids.
HIM: Yes, some do! (He insisted).
HER: Yes, some do, but some do not (as calmly as she could).
HIM: (Somewhat agitated) But some do! You need kids so you can play with them and have fun with in them the living room—watching TV and playing games.

Fortunately, Mr. Wonderful had to leave the table to go to the back to finish getting dressed for the wedding. Yet, the conversation left the lovely lady feeling a little exasperated.

While calming herself from the unexpected twist in the conversation, the lovely lady thought, 'why am I arguing with a five-year-old about this very personal matter?' With that simple question, she managed to recover a bit as she smiled at the hilarious thought of it. However, again struggling to keep her mind in check, she started wondering if he were right and she really did miss out on something by not having that experience. Then, still back in recovery mode, she thought, "What does he know? He still needs help getting dressed."

The back and forth of the internal dialogue seemed to continue longer than she had hoped. Her conversation with him was not the first time she would have to beat back the bludgeoning thoughts of the 'what-ifs' or the soppy sadness and anxieties of the 'what-could-have-been(s)'. Yet, the struggle continued and this time she seemed to be losing.

But as it were, whenever the struggle reached a breaking point; whenever it started to seem like all the insecure thoughts and notions that she had previously taken captive, began rioting in her mind and crushing in on her—that is when the mystery lady approached and made her presence known.

As the mystery lady descended into the lovely lady's personal struggle, the scene was set for a very important, figurative, yet very deep heart-to-heart conversation. She approached from the right-hand side and hovered above as if in the lovely lady's own consciousness. Then, without asking permission, she leaned in and held the lovely lady close. And, on queue but in her own time, she reassured the lovely lady with words of warmth and affection, speaking to her in a language that it seems only the two of them would understand. As this was happening, the lovely lady was becoming so captivated by the presence, that the raging battle that was taking place in her mind about her past and present, seemed to come to a screeching halt.

> HER: Do I know you?
> MYSTERY LADY: Yes, we have met many, many times before.
> HER: We have? Why can I not recall an occasion?
> MYSTERY LADY: It is not unusual that people forget.
> HER: Are you here for the bride or the groom?
> MYSTERY LADY: My dear lady, I am here for anyone who needs me.
> HER: I noticed your presence in the room a while ago.
> MYSTERY LADY: Yes, but I saw you first and I have never taken my eyes off you.
> HER: I do not understand; why would you watch over me in such a way?
> MYSTERY LADY: Because you invite me. Now enough; let us talk about you.
> HER: But...
> MYSTERY LADY: Silence, please. Let us talk about you.
> HER: Okay...but ...
> MYSTERY LADY: Why are you struggling with this?
> HER: Do you mean the little boy?
> MYSTERY LADY: No, not the little boy; the villains in your mind.
> HER: Well, if you had heard the whole conversation, you would...
> MYSTERY LADY: I did, and I do.
> HER: (Sigh). It was like I have been sitting through a real-life version of the song, 'Killing Me Softly.'
> MYSTERY LADY: (Smiles). You are so dramatic.

HER: But I thought I had put all that nonsense behind me. I thought I had come to terms with the fact that the life that I am living now is my life, no matter what else I had hoped or imagined. Now I have this kid trying to make me feel like I did not try hard enough; that I did things all wrong; and that I am missing out on something.

MYSTERY LADY: Somehow, you never really put things behind you; you just put them out of mind or replaced those things with something else. You must be careful when deciding what that something else is. It must be bigger than yourself and bigger than whatever 'unpleasant' situation you might encounter. And, you must commit to staying focused on that something else because there will always be people, places, or things, that will—how do you say? —come for you. And besides that, your little Mr. Wonderful is just a kid who happens to think you are pretty great.

HER: I know, but he said…

MYSTERY LADY: He said you are special. In fact, he said that you are so awesome and so special that he cannot imagine you not having kids of your own. Did you hear anything else that I said?

HER: He did?

MYSTERY LADY: That is what I gleaned from the conversation.

HER: Yes, I heard the other things that you said too, and I know you are right. But, sometimes my "something else" makes me feel more forsaken than loved. Maybe not as much as I used to, but I do still have some unanswered questions in my head, especially when I look at the lives of many of my friends and family and start thinking about my not…

MYSTERY LADY: Listen. Your life is your life. It might look different than the next person's or it might not live up to the expectations of another, but who can judge you when most (like you) are questioning whether they have correctly figured things out for themselves?

HER: I know, but how; why do some...

MYSTERY LADY: You are holding the hand you were dealt; play it to the best of your abilities.

HER: I believe—at least before that conversation—I believed that I was at least playing poker, but right now, I feel like I am playing a very challenging game of solitaire, or better yet—Old Maid. It is like I have missed something or someone.

MYSTERY LADY: Yes, it might seem that you have missed opportunities, but how do you know whether if missing those other opportunities might have saved you from other burdens, headaches, or heartaches that you might not have been able to bear?

HER: But I have many burdens now, even so.

MYSTERY LADY: Yes, and you will. You see, all the "burdens"—or opportunities for growth—that might be in store for you are not necessarily revealed at one time; but you can rest assured that we are only allowed to take part in those that you can bear.

HER: Wait... did you just say "we"?

MYSTERY LADY: My dear lady, be thankful not only for your life but also for the opportunities that you have allowed and accepted in your life. No matter whatever else you think you might have desired: those are yours alone and not anyone else's.

HER: (After reflection). Yes! Yes, you are right.

MYSTERY LADY: Yes. Now take these words to heart: You are an overcomer—just like the characters in that movie that you have been recasting in your mind.

HER: Wait! How did you know about that?

MYSTERY LADY: I guess it was written all over your face. Now go in peace, back to your happy place (as she sauntered away).

HER: Wait. What is your name?

MYSTERY LADY: (Walking away but never losing eye contact she said) my name is Grace and I am a gift to you.

As she watched Grace saunter around the room to undoubtedly rest upon the shoulders of another soul in need, the lovely lady started to remember the earlier encounters that they shared. And, as she started to recall, though embarrassed, she started feeling relieved to recollect that in those encounters, Grace appeared equally as amazing, but distinctly different in each.

"That explains why I did not recognize her," she thought. Then she thought, "no, that is not a good enough excuse." Then, after glancing around the room and putting names to familiar faces; she found another face in the small crowd that she scantly recognized. But, after taking a closer look and then listening closely to hear his voice, the lovely lady realized that he was none other than old Mr. Parker (a shade-tree mechanic who she remembers always covered in dirt and oil) that she has known since childhood.

"Mr. Parker looks great", she thought. He was clean and more dressed up than she ever remembered. At that moment, she almost shouted, 'AHA!' That was at the exact moment that the lovely lady realized that the shame was not in her not recognizing Grace; the shame was in her beating herself up about it and not realizing that just like Mr. Parker, Grace might look different in different situations.

Feeling more relieved she beamed, 'Now let's get this wedding started,' as she, at the same time, sprung to her feet to go over to meet and greet the so-far assembled guests before heading to the back to lend a helping hand.

Chapter 7

Grace - The Total Package

It turned out to be a very long but beautiful day. The wedding ceremony had come to its end, and the reception was winding down. While preparing to leave, the lovely lady reflected on the opportunities she had to reconnect with some family and friends that she had not seen in a while, and to meet new people that she had not before known—including a charming, little fella that managed to innocently challenge everything that she had trained herself to believe about her life. And in that, she survived what seemed a conversation from the abyss. Yet, before it was all over, she remembered the beautiful—but often-times—overlooked, presence of amazing Grace, which proved to be a gift of God.

T. T. Carole

Girl's Imagination Gone Wild

Now back in her car after helping to secure the couple's mountains of gifts and well-wishes, and heading home for some rest and relaxation, the lovely lady set her attention back to Grace. She realized that even if there were not a physical presence of Grace in the room, whenever she found herself in a tricky situation, the divine presence abounded.

What if I were to direct a biopic about her and had to create a physical likeness for her; what would she look like and what would she be like?" she wondered.

"Girl, your imagination and creative juices are really flowing today," she chuckled to herself. Nevertheless, that did not stop her from a further examination of the prospect of doing so.

"Okay, let's go", she thought. "If I were to write a movie about Grace as I have experienced her, who would play the lead?" she quizzed. Then reflectively she felt a heaviness in her heart as she realized the enormity of the role verses the fundamental insufficiencies present in the human experience, which would disqualify practically anyone from playing the part.

"But that is what actors do; they act", she thought. "In fact, that is what most reasonable people do: we act like we have sense; act like we care; act like things are okay; or..., the list goes on."

She then regained hope in the possibilities and continued to pursue her entertaining thoughts.

Sailing through traffic, yet still several miles from home, she began setting the scene in her mind. She remained pleasantly uninterrupted in her thoughts, however, until shortly after entering the highway, where she started experiencing stop-and-go traffic.

There was—what looked like—a severe incident on the road between where she was, and her planned exit. "I pray that everything is okay there," she thought while glimpsing the multitude of lights that were glaring from the many emergency vehicles ahead.

At this point, the first responders had already aided the occupants of the involved vehicles and were in the stage of clearing the debris from the road. She discerned this was the case because after inching along for about a quarter of a mile, traffic suddenly came to a complete stop.

"Ugh!" she sighed in frustration. Then knowing she was not going anywhere soon, she calmed herself by wondering aloud, "How should I describe Grace?"

She then started thinking:

> I know that Grace is the personification of the attributes of God, therefore does not have a physical form, but most people do not understand things that they do not see. So, if I am producing a biopic, I would like to present Grace in a way that is conceptually true and—at the same time—surprisingly relatable.

She then recalled a word that she had heard before that would help her with the process: anthropomorphically.

"Now, that is a mouthful," she thought as she laughed aloud. If there was one thing that the lovely lady was extremely good at, it was, unapologetically, keeping herself entertained.

"Hey Google, what is the meaning of anthropomorphically?" she playfully asked her android. "Anthropomorphically is the act of ascribing human form or attributes to a being or thing not human, especially to a deity," the clearly-spoken, but robot-like voice answered.

"Of all the simple words that tend to escape my mind these days; how do I remember that one?" she thought as she shook her head. "Well, at the rate this traffic is moving, I will have plenty of time to think of a lot more like it."

Fifty

Still stuck in her thought as much as she is in traffic, the lovely lady started reflecting on her many encounters with Grace. She started remembering that Grace not only saved her but is also shielding her. She started remembering situations when Grace covered her whenever it seemed like she was falling short while relying on her own strength, or while still all messed up inside. She started remembering incidences when Grace concealed her from people or things that were no good for her. And she started having reassuring thoughts about how Grace is perfecting her and making her suitable for Paradise, while at the same time protecting her like a rare treasure that—in time—will be delivered, safely, to the King.

"Wow! Grace is so divinely perfect. How many expressions of beauty should I use to ascribe to the likeness of her?" she wondered.

"At the very least, I should use one for each year of my life—but I do not plan on being in the car for that long," she chuckled.

She then thought to direct the question to Google®: "Hey Google®. What symbol or number is associated with grace?" The very pleasant Google® voice responded loud and clear: "In numerology, fifty normally symbolizes grace, kindness, and regeneration."

"There's that number fifty again!" she exclaimed aloud. "If I see or hear the number 50 one more time before I get home, then that will be confirmation."

She was quite amused at the thought. However—if there were such a thing—while looking up to assess the progress of the traffic that stood still ahead of her, it seemed by some strange coincidence that she noticed the license plate on the car in the right lane and slightly ahead of her read: B4E-GL5O. "Well I'll be darn. That is close enough; then fifty it will be."

Even while accepting her own challenge to create such a thing, she was thinking about how difficult her self-appointed task would be. "This is going to be way more difficult than recasting the story of Ruth movie." However, nudged by a thought, she decided maybe not because though never expressly mentioned in the telling of the stories, Grace was present and deeply embedded in each of their lives.

"My goodness," she declared aloud to herself. "I guess if you think about it, Grace has been around and working for eternity.

In fact, there is a great cloud of witnesses to which I can refer that should be able to help to make this challenge easier".

Expressions of Beauty

"Oh, how I hate being stuck in traffic," she complained. "Hey, if you want to get over then use your blinker. I am here; I own this lane; you cannot just take it! IDIOT!" she yelled into her windshield.

"Why is he or she an idiot?" she asked herself remorsefully. "Girl, you need to calm down; it is not that serious".

She started thinking to herself about how she was so grateful for Grace. "If Grace were a person she would never have yelled such things at that person," she thought while thinking to herself about how she would be a totally lost little chicken head without it.

Subsequently, after managing to pardon the infraction, she felt more enthused to communicate the very influential and winsome qualities of such a powerful force as Grace.

She then traveled back into the creative studio of her mind and started fashioning the figure; thinking:

> The face of Grace has a pure radiance. It is an unadulterated beauty that is never flaunted. In fact, she typically tries to appear so simple and undemanding that she could easily blend into a crowd with as much ease as possible, but even so, still ends up the most beautiful wall flower in the room.
>
> In stature, Grace is petite, agile, and yet sufficient enough to operate in a way to bring healing in the small, dark, hidden

spaces in the heart and mind. And at the same time, Grace is stately enough to stand as a shield between the Father's wrath and the object of her desire.

Her neck is stout and strong, because Grace works under the full weight of the Head—who is greater than eternity.

The shoulders of Grace are broad, which allows her to grin and bear the slights of those who only recognize her in times of need; and remain—while forgotten all over again—even when the urgency of the need subsides.

Her chest is big and busty because Grace is built to hold a humongous heart that distributes enough forgiveness to right wrongs; and enough love to cover a multitude of faults.

Her arms are respectively long and exceptionally strong, because with those arms Grace saves, embraces, and protects even some who might seem unredeemable.

Her hands and fingers are equitably long, because with them, Grace fans the flames of love, joy, peace, patience, kindness, goodness, and faithfulness—not only as needed but in all times—to help temper negative impulses.

Someone behind her honks a horn, and the jarring sound interrupts her train of thought: honk, honk. "Oh goodie; traffic is moving again, and it is a good thing because I really have to go," the lovely lady thought as she was nearing a panic. "I should have made that last trip before I left the banquet hall!"

Her thoughts then transitioned to an article she remembered reading, which suggests that a full bladder can cloud a person's mind or decrease their judgment to an extent like the effects of consuming a few ounces of an alcoholic beverage over a brief period of time.

That explains little Mr. Wonderful's first remarks to her, she thought while smiling and shaking her head at the thought of him.

"Well, I had better concentrate on the roads", she thought; "I would hate to be the cause of or be caught up in an incident like what just happened". Then, with a cautious determination, she gripped the stirring wheel; looked to focus on what was happening around her; drove carefully to her planned exit, and then a few more blocks down the road; and finally parked safely in the comforts of her garage.

Pardon the Interruption

"Hello?" she said as she answered the phone while preparing herself for the hike up the stairs and to the nearest powder room.

It was her brother on the other end of the phone, calling (after hearing about the incident on the highway) to make sure she made it home okay.

"Yes, I made it home safely, thank the Lord."

"Yes, everything turned out nicely," she replied.

"No problem, any time. I am happy that I could help," she responded.

"Okay, but …"

"Um huh; um huh; okay, but …"

"Okay, but you are going to have to let me off this phone before you think you are talking to a drunken sailor," she joked.

She did not know if he had a clue as to what she was talking about, but she did find that no matter what he was thinking, he correctly took the hint that he needed to end his conversation.

"I will be sure to call you back sometime early next week, okay? Okay, bye!"

"Now I can concentrate on getting up those steps before the flood water breaches the wall," she chuckled.

The Craving

"Why am I so hungry? It is not like I did not get enough to eat at the reception," she thought while changing into more comfortable clothing and contemplating how she would spend the rest of the evening.

She went to the kitchen to chase down a light snack, which she decided would be heavily buttered, microwave popcorn accompanied by a tall glass of ginger ale over ice, with a twist of lime and a fresh sprig of mint. "Now, that is good," she said after taking the first sip.

She stood next to the counter to watch over the bag of popcorn that was starting to hiss and swell in the microwave. The sound of the popping corn triggered her thoughts, and she began toying with the idea of assigning something for which she is very thankful to each kernel of corn as it popped. This made her smile and she started the exercise—that is until the kernels started exploding at a pace with which she could not keep up.

"Well, that was fun," she thought as she waited for the bag to cool a bit before pulling it out and opening it to pour on the melted butter.

Before too long, she retrieved the bag of popped corn from the microwave. Then, while pouring on the butter and shaking the bag to get an even distribution of the expected goodness, her mood changed from thanksgiving to melancholy as she took note of what she was doing.

"Life is strange," she thought. "Sometimes, even those popped up blessing for which one might be so thankful can get rained on (sometimes it seems from above) and turn into slippery situations."

And then, as if suddenly bestowed a new line of thinking, she once again beamed with pleasure as she thought about how delicious that popcorn was going to taste.

Ultimately, as she became more settled in her mind, she said to herself very contently, "Yeah, we might get rained on unexpectedly and shaken up a bit sometimes; but in the end, if we remain firmly in the Maker's hands through the melt downs and turbulence, we will find that it was all just preparation for some major goodness that is yet to come."

The Obsession

Now settled in with her snack and readying herself for some rest and relaxation—and watching whatever was playing on television—the lovely lady plops onto the loveseat. As she tucked her feet under and buried her bottom into the softness of the mega cushions, she again set the wheels of her mind in motion and started thinking some more about Grace—because for some reason, she could not get enough.

Soon into her thoughts, though, she realized that she had not finished casting the actor who would star in her imaginary Netflix® biopic; nor had she finished the 50-point description that she had begun in her challenge.

"Let me see; she could have a face as pretty as..., no, not her—nice face but judging from all reports, a highly unsuitable personality," she thought. "Then, how about..., nope—too plastic," she rebuffed. "Okay, then how about..., nah, very pretty, but she exudes too much simplicity and not enough elegance," she protested.

"This is getting way too complicated," she thought while starting to feel a little overwhelmed and frustrated by the depth and breadth of her self-created challenge. She then considered approaching the task from a different angle.

"Maybe the lead actor's looks should not have anything to do with the telling of the story," she thought while images on her muted television started eliciting from her a surprisingly different opinion of an actor whom she formerly thought to be—according to conventionally adopted standards—less than average in appearance.

The camera lingered on the actor's face during what seemed like an intense moment in the scene. Without hearing the words spoken, the lovely lady watched intently as the character's expression changed from relative calm to all-out outrage. This change did not happen instantaneously; it occurred over a period which lasted up to a minute and a half or two.

The scene, because of the expertise of production, allows the audience the opportunity to experience the full depth of the character's raw emotions. And, as the camera focused in on her face, it was obvious that she was playing a role not of a beauty queen, but of a regular, hard-working woman who had stumbled into an unpleasant situation. She was not polished, plastic, nor elegant—just a real lady who captured the attention of at least this audience of one and made her feel deeply not only for the character but also for what the character was experiencing.

Drawn in, the lovely lady's attention fixed on the character's tear-filled eyes, because the angle of the camera demanded it; and in doing so, she could not help but notice how naturally attractive and nicely shaped they were.

"Even the brutal focus of a zoomed lens could not take that away from her", the lovely lady thought.

As it were, the character was in the middle of a monologue; therefore, the camera seemed to linger at that awkwardly revealing angle for some time. This gave the lovely lady an opportunity for further examination. So, without unmuting the sound, she began making other assessments—not about what was happening in the scene, but about the actor who was playing the role of the character and also of her own thoughts, attitudes, and feelings.

"Are you really going to be that petty-minded?" she asked herself before dismissing that question with a quick retort: "It is not petty-mindedness if there is no intent of malice. In fact, this might be as much about me as it is about her."

After assessing her eyes, the lovely lady then unleashed the fullness of her curiosity to wander about the face—as the camera directed—and finally landed her attention on the actor's nose.

Her nose—which some of her critics complain is too large, oddly shaped, or unattractive—she agreed was rather large, or (more gently put) very prominent. Yet after reconciling that single feature with all her other well-formed or oddly bodacious ones, she thought aloud to herself, "Her nose fills her face perfectly; I could not imagine it being any different. Lord I hope she does not change it."

"What show, or movie am I watching?" she snapped. "That is okay, I do not want to know because I do not need another distraction," she then thought to herself before returning to her careful consideration of the actor's features.

Before the scene would come to an end, the lovely lady had successfully completed a full assessment of the face of this person, who often is (for the wrong reason) the subject of "Beautiful People Weekly"—if there were such a thing. She decided that not only were the actor's individual features—her eyes, nose, lips, her coloring, and even the shape of her face—very distinct, but together they made her uniquely beautiful, just as God had planned.

After partaking in that exercise, the lovely lady received more clarity about the biopic project that was going on in her head. She realized that she had been obsessing more about the physical appearance of the actor for the starring role, than of the representation of the subliminal manifestation of true Grace in terms of enriching lives or influencing effective outreach. This revelation, however, did not make her task any easier; yet she persisted.

She then sat straight up on the loveseat, placed her feet firmly on the floor, grabbed her remote to turn off the television, and went back to the challenge of redeeming Grace as a character in her imaginary biopic.

Redeeming Grace

Slurping through the last of her deliciously refreshing drink, and solidly refocusing on her effort to complete her challenge, the lovely lady began to conclude in her mind: "The divine attribute of Grace is magnificent; however, it radiates as beautifully from a simple, plain Jane or country bumpkin as it does a carnally-desired, raven-haired beauty."

She nodded in agreement.

Happy about her renewed, informed thinking, she then concluded with a couple more thoughts about how looks are so artificial; and as far as another's spiritual acceptance or awareness; who can really judge the heart of another?

The flood gates were now open, which led to a short internal debate in support of at least one of those thoughts: "Yes, we can judge actions, but we all can be bad actors at one time or another."

She then settled in her mind that the best person for the starring role should have no majesty nor beauty of form that would make her desirable or appealing to the masses, and further that, that is exactly the type needed to produce the most undeniable good deed.

Realizing she was finally getting it, she then leaned back into the comfort of the surrounding cushions and thought to herself:

> I like the beautiful actor in that show or movie that was just on because like Grace; on the surface, her beauty might be contrary to human thinking; however, once accepted for who she is, and her true beauty watchfully studied and revealed, she is sure to become the standard on which all could hang their hope.

Then vividly recalling the features of the actor, she wondered how she could use her features to complete a description that exudes the beauty of a redeeming Grace.

"Redeeming! That is a powerful word, she thought. "Alexa, what is the definition of 'redeeming'?"

"Redeeming: Compensating for some fault or defect," the gentle voice returned.

Believing she had struck gold, she thought to start just as she first observed of the actor—with the eyes. And, with that thought, her mind's eye began imagining:

> Characteristically, she has very large, bright, deep-set eyes that are proportionate to the Head, because the eyes of Grace always seek to find a lonely and hopeless soul, one who could benefit from an undeserved gift of comfort and joy. The eyes of Grace find beauty in every soul and do not lead her to judge people by artificial, generally-accepted standards.

T. T. Carole

Her ears are noticeably delicate, but are firm and well-defined, because Grace listens for the exact moment of submission—when she is invited to come in—and then she shows up with perfect timing.

Grace's mouth is prominently large. She has full lips with a well-defined bow that pecks the spirit, and a smooth pliable tongue that can lasso the Word and perfects her whisper. This because the mouth of Grace allows her to speak softly into the hearts and minds the assurance of the Gospel of Christ to all who have ears to hear.

Her nose is both long and broad because the nose of Grace does a smell check to make sure that her beloveds are emanating sweet, life-giving aromas that are pleasing to God.

Because of her perfect beauty, Grace does not need makeup; however, she tucks some items away to carry with her in case of an emergency. So, in her bosom, Grace carries salve on a blood-stained cloth to apply to new, stinging wounds and bruises; and concealer to cover old scars of hurt and pain.

Her clothes—though from goodwill—are elegant and fit her perfectly but are yet designed and crafted as one-size-fits-all, because Grace will lend even her best: cloak as cover for weaknesses; shoes for walking in the light; undergarments for strengthening the will; hat for enlightening the mind; and accessories for providing shields of protection.

The Gift of Grace

"And, I do believe that makes 50," the lovely lady concluded before leaning back to ruminate over those things that she had thought.

Not realizing how tiring the entire day had been for her, it was not long after leaning back before she started to doze off. However, before she allowed sleep to overtake her, she suddenly had an alarming thought that caused her to sit straight up and then leap into action.

"Oh, my goodness! I did not write any of that down," she exclaimed while looking up and raising both hands into the air as if in full surrender to the thoughts in her head, her better angels, or her Creator and Higher Power.

Over the years, the lovely lady had become very conscientious about keeping good notes about her facts of life (her experiences) and she cultivated a habit of keeping journals from which she could draw during downtimes, or during her times of meditation, reflection and thanksgiving.

She journals faithfully about almost any event in her life—specially to capture those moments when something happens that she thinks is very significant. Thus, the events of this day and its many twists and turns, she decided, would certainly qualify as one worthy of memorializing.

Without further hesitation, she leaped from the loveseat to fetch her laptop, which was not too far away. Once plugged in and ready to go, she mused a bit about how to capture her thoughts about the day that was, before surrendering them to that fuzzy place of no return.

So, to not miss a thing, she started replaying in her mind the events of the day, including everything from the non-event of waking up and preparing for the day, to her ending the day where she was now: finishing her self-prescribed challenge of describing and casting the essence of Grace for her imaginary biopic.

From one event to the other, she thought about how to capture the most significant of them in meaningful ways.

She thought about arriving at the banquet hall, and then searched for any significance there.

She thought about meeting little Mr. Wonderful and noted the ramifications.

She thought about the actors she envisioned, and them successfully rendering a realistic portrayal of the characters that they would take on, in her version of the telling of the Story of Ruth; then typed a few notes.

Then, she thought about the wedding ceremony for the new couple, and blushed while thinking about their new, marital bliss.

She thought about the incident she met on the highway on the way home and felt concerned about what might have happened; then typed a short prayer for all who might have been involved.

Finally, after thinking about everything else, she, again, circled back to Grace.

Considering all the implications of the events of the day, she hunched over her laptop and started typing words fashioned after the famous lyrics of John Newton (1779):

IT WAS GRACE THAT BROUGHT ME SAFE THUS FAR, AND GRACE WILL LEAD ME ON.

APPENDIX - A Guide for Personal Application

But he said to me, "My grace is sufficient for you, for my power is made perfect in weakness." Therefore, I will boast all the more gladly about my weaknesses, so that Christ's power may rest on me." 2 Cor. 12:9

The short studies that follow are designed for individual or small group analysis to supplement the narratives contained within and support added opportunities for exploring and further considering the supernatural workings of God, and the provisions of his amazing grace.

You are encouraged to try and answer all the questions in this guide on a personal basis. There are no right or wrong answers; however, if answering any of these causes you any discomfort, ask the Holy Spirit for guidance. Pray and try again—over and over again—until you are comfortable with the truth of your answer.

GUIDE TO PERSONAL APPLICATION

Discussion Questions for Chapter 1

Focus Verse: "But by the grace of God, I am what I am, and his grace to me was not without effect." 1 Corinthians 15:10

DNA tests have come a long way in helping us to identify our human lineage; however, what they cannot help us identify is God's purpose for our lives. Discovering our purpose requires that we first know who God is and then begin building a relationship with him so that he can guide us by his spirit, and according to His word. It also requires that we are willing to examine ourselves and truthfully evaluate our behavior against his standards.

1. Which version of the sophisticated lady would describe the lovely lady in this chapter, and why?
2. Which version would describe you, and why?
3. Cinderella used her imaginations as a means of coping or escaping from unpleasant situations. Is this a healthy practice? Why or why not?
4. This chapter suggests that over the years, the lovely lady learned to accept the fact that her life did not turn out as she had hoped; yet she persisted. How would accepting some things that we might not be able to change make our lives more comfortable?
5. In the focus verse, the Apostle Paul is speaking to how, because of God's grace, his encounter with Jesus changed his life. What does Paul's encounter tell us about God desire for humanity?

GUIDE TO PERSONAL APPLICATION

Discussion Questions for Chapter 2

Focus Verse: "One who loves a pure heart and who speaks with grace will have a king for a friend." Proverbs 22:11

One of the most phenomenal conveniences to date seems to be the cell phone device (android or smart phone) that allows us to connect to the world from any location, and at any time of day or night. The camera is a very popular feature on these devices—whether for taking selfies, or filming events and sharing them either in real-time, or by video on a larger platform. It seems that no matter where you go or what you might be doing, there is a real probability that someone is watching.

1. In Chapter 1, the lovely lady sense that someone was watching over her; however, that did not give her a reason for alarm. What was it about the presence that might have kept the lovely lady from being afraid?
2. How might we conduct ourselves differently if we knew for sure that someone was watching us always? Why?
3. While recreating the story of Ruth in her mind, the lovely lady seemed obsessed with putting the characters' raw emotions on full display. Other than for telling a more compelling story, why might this be so important to her?
4. In the focus verse above, what might be the benefit of having a king for a friend?
5. What does it mean to speak with grace?

GUIDE TO PERSONAL APPLICATION

Discussion Questions for Chapter 3

Focus Verse: "Therefore, with minds that are alert and fully sober, set your hope on grace to be brought to you when Jesus Christ is revealed in his coming." 1 Peter 1:13

Whether joyous occasions or tragic events, life is full of circumstances that could cloud our judgement and cause us to lose track of important things we should value, or moments we should treasure. Our emotions are a gift that we can engage freely; however, our best decisions are best made—not in moments of passion, hilarity, nor doom—but after careful, prayerful deliberation.

1. In this chapter, the lovely lady seemed willing to take on the challenge of engaging with Mr. Wonderful despite warnings. What sign did she receive that she might have been heading for trouble?
2. Is being intuitive the same as having faith? Why or why not?
3. The lovely lady's version of the story of Ruth that she was crafting in her mind told of Orpah's having to decide about her life after a tragic event. Based on what we know, did Orpah make the right decision? Why or why not?
4. The Focus Verse suggests that a knowledge of Christ brings grace. Is it suggesting now, or in the future?
5. How does one get knowledge of Christ?

GUIDE TO PERSONAL APPLICATION

Discussion Questions for Chapter 4

Focus Verse: "Let your conversation be always full of grace seasoned with salt, so that you may know how to answer everyone." Colossians 4:6

Nearing the end their time of service in the office of President of the United States, First Lady Michelle Obama (Barrack) gifted us words of wisdom about handling adversity, saying: "When they go low, we go high." That is a great prescription for reaching the right frame of mind for handling difficult moments or contentious conversations.

1. In this chapter, the lovely lady was alarmed by the critic's review of Ruth's characterization in the movie version of the story. According to the critic, Ruth was portrayed as one with a sassy attitude towards Boaz, and the lovely lady disagreed. In real life, is it best to show an attitude of pride or one of humility –especially in times of need? Why?
2. Is humility a sign of weakness? Why or why not?
3. According to what we might know about Ruth, why did her actions speak louder than her words?
4. According to what we know, who else took notice of Ruth's actions? Why?
5. Like it or not, we all stand to be judged by our words or deeds. What is more important: words, actions, or both? Why?

GUIDE TO PERSONAL APPLICATION

Discussion Questions for Chapter 5

Focus Verse: "And the God of all grace, who called you to his eternal glory in Christ, after you have suffered a little while, will himself restore you and make you strong, firm and steadfast." 1 Peter 5:10

One of Aesop's Fables tells of a dog with a bone in his mouth who, dropped his bone in pond and lost it after inadvertently dropping the bone while trying to seize the bone belonging to another dog, which happened to be his own reflection in the water. While hoping that the dog did not starve to death after the incident, we are hopeful that he or she learned a valuable lesson.

1. In the chapter, the lovely lady invested a lot of her time and efforts to make herself attractive to Mr. Wonderful even though she learned that he only wanted one thing from her. How did she set herself up for whatever was coming next—whether good or bad?
2. Sometimes we desire people or things that are either not intended for us or is not good for us. How can we temper those desires?
3. When we are hurt by our own choices, what is the best route for the fastest recovery?
4. We all make mistakes at some point in life, sometimes causing us to suffer through a period of guilt and shame How does God view our mistakes?
5. What mechanism does God employ to help us to recover from those mistakes?

GUIDE TO PERSONAL APPLICATION

Discussion Questions for Chapter 6

Focus Verse: "They are a garland to grace your head and a chain to adorn your neck." Proverbs 1:9

From Proverbs of antiquity; to the sitcom, "Father Knows Best", which first began airing almost 70 years ago; to the long-running Dear Abby advice column, which has been in print for over 60 years; to the well-known soul original, "Grandma Hands", which was written and performed by Bill Withers almost 50 years ago; to an R&B favorite hit titled, "Momma Used to Say" which blew up the charts and was performed by the artist known as Junior almost 40 years ago. They all espouse a belief that taking advice from an authority figure could be very beneficial to the receiver.

1. How is Grace represented in this chapter?
2. After little Mr. Wonderful upset the lovely lady's apple cart in this chapter, grace came to her rescue. How did Grace help to save the day for her?
3. What was some of the best advice that Grace gave the lovely lady in this chapter?
4. Why did the lovely lady not recognize Grace whenever she first saw her?
5. The lovely lady compared her not recognizing Grace to her not readily recognizing Mr. Parker whom she has known since her childhood. How is this explained?

GUIDE TO PERSONAL APPLICATION

Discussion Questions for Chapter 7

Focus Verse: "Each of you should use whatever gift you have received to serve others, as faithful stewards of God's grace in its various forms." 1 Peter 4:10

The greatest reward of one who has shopped for hours on end to find a perfect gift, is to see its recipient appreciating the gift and using it to in some way to enhance their life. Grace is a gift from God. Because His gift to us is more perfect than any that we could ever receive from another mortal being, He expects that we appreciate it for what it is and use it in our daily lives in a way that would magnify and glorify Him.

1. We might sometimes find ourselves in situations that seem untenable and it leave us wondering, "Where is God?" How does God communicate that he is near to us, especially in times of trials?
2. God has a unique way of speaking to his children to reassure us, lead and guide us, or to rebuke us. What is this special form of communication, and how do we know when it is His voice?
3. We, by nature, tend to judge people and things by comparing them to other people and things that we see. What might be a better standard for making such judgements? Why/

GUIDE TO PERSONAL APPLICATION

4. Though there are different gifts and types of gifts. How is finding and working in our area of giftedness a means of self-enrichment and a way of glorifying God?
5. What is your gift, and if you have discovered it; how are how are you using it?

About The Author

Sometimes it takes dusting off the cobwebs and emptying her 30-year old trousseau before a woman realizes and enjoys the fact that she was born to be that favorite, rich aunt. ~ T. T. Carole

The author graduated from Columbia College, St. Louis, MO, with a B.A. in General Studies with a minor in Business. She also graduated from Missouri Baptist University, St. Louis, MO, with a Certificate of Ministry and Leadership; and has earned diplomas and certifications in teaching through the Evangelical Training Association (ETA); Christian Counseling and Coaching, and Extraordinary Women Ministry Studies through Light University (powered by the American Association of Christian Counselors (AACC)); interior decorating and design through PCS School of Design; and a list of others. She is a life-long member of Friendly Temple Missionary Baptist Church, St. Louis, MO.

Her life's experience has been richly rewarded by her multifaceted background as a professional in Corporate America; a business owner and operator in the world of interior design; and as a student, coach, teacher, and motivational speaker in ministry and religious studies.

Her love for educating herself; her passion for inspiring and sharing with others; and her desire to do the work that she believes God intended for her to do, have converged and culminated, for her, into a thirst for creative expression as a writer.

In this profession, her greatest desire and mission is to engage the readers in various forums and on many levels and by presenting complex, spiritual ideas in an interesting, Biblically-aligned, and creative format.

Whether reading along for enjoyment; embarking on learning a new skill or craft; or, simply needing to know that you are not alone in your experience, this author sure has something just for you.

Additional Titles From T. T. Carole

Designed for Life – Sipping Tea in the Living Room is the first of the self-help series that not only leads the reader through a spiritual assessment, but also share real-life interior design principles and techniques that are very useful for setting up home.

Available at Amazon.com and as noted in Contact Information that follows

Dishing Soul Food in the Kitchen is the second installment in the Designed for Life series. Again, the self help content is spiritually uplifting as it assesses the human condition in various circumstances, and practical as it gives real-life home engineering principles and techniques that are sure to add value to the life of the readers.

Available at Amazon.com and as noted in Contact Information that follows.

Contact Information

We would love to hear from you. Please look for and connect with T. T. Carole on the following social media sites:

- On her website at: abeautyfilledlife.com

- On Facebook® at: @teeteecarole

- On Instagram® at: abeautyfilledlife

- On Twitter® at: abeautyfilledlife@ABFL

- Email her at: abeautyfilledlife@gmail.com

www.ingramcontent.com/pod-product-compliance
Lightning Source LLC
Chambersburg PA
CBHW060340080526
44584CB00013B/857